Rebecca Gilman

blue surge

Rebecca Gilman is the recipient of the Prince Prize for Commissioning Original Work for *Blue Surge*, which premiered at the Goodman Theatre in July 2001. Her plays include *Spinning into Butter*, *Boy Gets Girl* (both of which were commissioned and originally produced by the Goodman Theatre), and *The Glory of Living*. *Spinning into Butter* received its New York premiere at the Lincoln Center Theatre. *Boy Gets Girl* was first produced in New York at the Manhattan Theatre Club and received a Drama Desk Award nomination for best new play. *The Glory of Living* was produced in London at the Royal Court and subsequently received the George Devine Award and the *Evening Standard* Award for Most Promising Playwright. It had its New York premiere at MCC Theater in October 2001. Ms. Gilman is also the recipient of a Guggenheim Fellowship, the Roger L. Stevens Award from the Kennedy Center Fund for New American Plays, and the Scott McPherson Award.

Also by Rebecca Gilman,

available from Faber and Faber

Boy Gets Girl

Spinning into Butter

The Glory of Living

blue surge

blue surge

a play by
Rebecca Gilman

Faber and Faber
New York • London

Faber and Faber, Inc.
An affiliate of Farrar, Straus and Giroux
19 Union Square West, New York 10003

Faber and Faber Ltd
3 Queen Square
London WC1N 3AU

Blue Surge was created with funds from the Prince Prize for Commissioning
Original Work, which was awarded to Rebecca Gilman and the Goodman
Theatre in 2000.

Library of Congress Cataloging-in-Publication Data
Gilman, Rebecca Claire.
    Blue surge : a play / by Rebecca Gilman.— 1st ed.
        p.   cm.
    ISBN 0-571-21107-0 (alk. paper)
        1. Teenage prostitution—Drama.   2. Prostitutes—Drama.   3. Middle
West—Drama.   4. Police—Drama.   I. Title.

PS3557.I456 B55 2001
812'.54—dc21

                                                            2001040876

Designed by Gretchen Achilles

10 9 8 7 6 5 4

To Charles

"What the bourgeoisie therefore produces, above all, are its own gravediggers. Its fall and the victory of the proletariat are equally inevitable."

—KARL MARX

blue surge

Cast of Characters

The world premiere of Blue Surge *was presented by the Goodman Theatre in Chicago, Illinois, on July 9, 2001. It was directed by Robert Falls. Sets were designed by Walt Spangler, costumes by Birgit Rattenborg Wise, lights by Michael Philippi, and sound by Richard Woodbury. The dramaturg was Tom Creamer, the production stage manager was Alden Vasguez, and the stage manager was Laxmi Kumaran. The cast was as follows:*

CURT   Joe Forbrich

SANDY   Rachel Miner

DOUG   Steve Key

HEATHER   Rebecca Jordan

BETH   Amy Landecker

Characters

CURT, *mid-thirties*

SANDY, *nineteen*

DOUG, *mid-thirties*

HEATHER, *mid-thirties*

BETH, *mid-thirties*

Time and Place

A mid-sized city in the Midwest, in the present

act one

Scene One

At rise: A room in a massage parlor, somewhere in the Mid-west, in the fall. There is a straight-backed chair and a platform, built to be a massage table but larger. The room is brightly lit and businesslike. A small boom box sits on a shelf next to some jars and bottles.

Curt and Sandy enter. Curt is fully dressed, a little nervous. Sandy wears a short silk robe and high heels. She is young, thin, and flat-chested, not a knockout at all.

SANDY Okay. Before we start the massage, I need you to sign this thing— *(Hands him a piece of paper.)*

CURT What is it?

SANDY Just a thing. *(He starts to read it. She looks at him.)* It just says that we're not responsible for any preexisting medical conditions. *(He's still reading.)* So, just basically, you need to sign it before we can get started.

CURT Okay. *(He signs it, hands it to her.)*

SANDY Okay— *(Looks at paper.)* Bill. I just gotta take this

out front, so why don't you go ahead and get undressed
and when I get back we'll get started.

CURT Okay.

(She exits. Curt looks around, then takes off his shoes,
shirt, pants. When he gets to his underwear he stops. He's
wearing briefs. He decides to leave them on. He sits down
on the chair and waits. Beat. Sandy returns. She takes a
look at him.)

SANDY You're going to leave your underwear on?

CURT Should I take them off?

SANDY No. However you're comfortable's fine. (Turns and
    looks vaguely at the shelf behind her.) Okay. Let me just
    find some oil here.

CURT Oil, huh? What are we going to use the oil for?

SANDY I'm going to rub it on your back.

CURT Oh. Well is there anything else you want to do
    with it?

SANDY No.

CURT Because oil can be sort of . . . you know, sensual.

SANDY Get on the table.

CURT Okay. (He lies down. Since it's not a real massage
    table, he has to keep his head up. Sandy starts

tentatively rubbing him. Takes the oil and squirts a lot on him.) Do you mind not putting so much on me? I don't want my shirt to stick to me.

SANDY Sorry.

CURT What's that smell?

SANDY The oil. It's called "spice."

CURT It smells like Bengay.

SANDY Yeah. I was wondering what it smelled like.

CURT It reminds of me of high school football. They were always rubbing it on you. If you ripped your arm off they'd rub Bengay on it.

SANDY Who'd you play for?

CURT Hewitt.

SANDY No way. I went to Huffman.

CURT Huffman? Huffman always kicked our ass.

SANDY Yeah, but our cheerleaders were cows.

(Beat. They're both self-conscious.)

CURT So, um, tell me . . . do you always just give massages?

SANDY That's our business. The fine art of therapeutic massage.

CURT Do you ever do anything . . . more intimate?

SANDY No. What kind of question is that?

CURT I just wondered how long you've been doing this.

SANDY Three months.

CURT Ow.

SANDY Did that hurt?

CURT Yes.

SANDY There's a knot in your back. Right there. *(She pokes at it.)*

CURT Ow!

SANDY How do you think that happened?

CURT It's a tension thing.

SANDY Well, you need to relax.

(Small beat.)

CURT Is there some way you could maybe help me relax?

SANDY I think that's what I'm doing. *(She rubs.)*

CURT Okay. But you know, sometimes you hear that you do other things in these places. Besides massages.

SANDY Look, mister, no matter what you hear, you're not going to get lucky with me. Okay?

(Beat.)

CURT Maybe I should go.

SANDY Maybe you should.

CURT *(He sits up. Looks at her.)* How old are you?

SANDY Twenty-one.

CURT No you're not. *(Beat. She crosses her arms.)* Okay. This clearly is not working out. I'll get dressed. *(He puts on his pants.)*

SANDY Do you want your money back?

CURT No. I took up your time. It's not your fault I'm a tight-ass.

SANDY I didn't say that.

CURT You didn't have to. *(Curt picks up his socks. Looks at one.)* My sock has a hole in it. *(Looks at Sandy.)* Let me just get my shoes on and I'll get out of your hair.

SANDY *(Laughs.)* God. I can't let you go.

CURT What?

SANDY You've got oil globbed up on your back. Let me just rub it in so it doesn't ruin your shirt.

CURT I don't know.

SANDY You don't have to lie down again, if you don't want.

CURT Okay. *(She rubs his back with the palms of her hands.)* Now that actually feels good.

SANDY If you want I could put some other kind of oil on. So you won't smell like Bengay. There's one that smells like coconut. It always reminds me of Panama City.

CURT Is that in Florida?

SANDY Yeah.

CURT I've never been to Florida.

SANDY No way. You should go.

CURT Well, I don't want to smell like coconut. *(She massages.)* So where did you train, to learn the fine art of therapeutic massage?

SANDY Nowhere. I'm what they call a natural. *(Beat. She rubs once more, then playfully shoves him forward.)* All done.

CURT *(Gets up, crosses to his clothes. She stands and watches.)* When's the last time you went to Florida?

SANDY I don't know. *(Beat.)* Senior year.

CURT When was that?

SANDY Last spring. Why?

CURT No reason. Just making conversation while I awkwardly get dressed.

SANDY *(Laughs. Beat.)* When I was a kid, when my mom'd take me to the doctor, if the doctor made me take my shirt off, my mom would take it and sit on it. Because it was always so cold in the doctor's office and he'd put that cold stethoscope on you and all. Then when the examination was over, my mom would hand me back my shirt and it'd be all warm, from where she was sitting on it.

CURT That was nice.

SANDY I always think something like that would be nice around here. Maybe a little warming oven or something. Or those heat lamps, like in restaurants. Then your clothes would be all toasty. *(Curt smiles, finishes getting dressed.)* I feel bad I didn't help your back at all.

CURT It's okay.

SANDY I don't know what I'm doing.

(Curt smiles sadly, shrugs.)

CURT It's okay. Neither do I.

Scene Two

The same room, a week later. Doug enters with Heather. Heather is wearing a teddy and high heels.

HEATHER You want a massage today, honey?

DOUG Yeah.

HEATHER Okay, you'll need to sign this form here. *(She finds a piece of paper, he signs without looking at it.)* Okay. Why don't you get undressed, and I'll take this up front, then when I come back, we can start.

DOUG Sweet.

(She exits. Doug strips completely without reservation, remains standing, naked. Heather enters.)

HEATHER Excellent. Now what would you like?

DOUG I don't know what I'm in the mood for today. What do you think we should do?

HEATHER Why don't you tell me what you want?

DOUG What can you offer?

HEATHER I don't want to make an offer, because sometimes people have different things in mind, then I offer up something and it sort of stymies their imagination.

DOUG You're cute.

HEATHER Thanks. What do you want to do?

DOUG Um, what about a full-release massage?

HEATHER Sure.

DOUG How much does that cost?

HEATHER Forty.

DOUG Oh. Well, what can I get for a hundred?

HEATHER A hundred can definitely buy you some fun.

DOUG Would you fuck me for a hundred?

HEATHER I'd fuck you for two.

DOUG Hey. What about anal?

HEATHER What about it?

DOUG If I gave you three hundred bucks, would you have anal sex with me?

HEATHER Well, sure, sweetie. I mean, normally, sure. But we might not want to do it today. If you know what I mean.

DOUG Why not?

HEATHER I'm not really clean. Down there.

DOUG Do you need to wipe?

HEATHER No. I need to do an enema. I haven't done an enema. So. What'll it be?

DOUG Oh! Well, um, hang on a second. *(He reaches for his pants, pulls out a wallet. Shows her his badge.)* Okay. What I really want is . . . you're under arrest for solicitation!

HEATHER *(Overlapping with "arrest.")* Oh, fuck me!

DOUG You have the right to remain silent.

HEATHER I didn't do anything!

DOUG *(Overlapping.)* Anything you say may be used against you in a court of law.

HEATHER You totally entrapped me! This was total entrapment!

DOUG *(Overlapping.)* You have the right to an attorney. If you cannot afford one—

HEATHER This is so fucking not gonna stick!

DOUG One will be appointed to you by the court.

HEATHER I can't believe this! I'm calling my lawyer right now. You picked the wrong person to fuck with, buddy.

DOUG Do you understand these rights as they have been read to you?

HEATHER Fuck you. You don't have anything on me.

DOUG Oh yeah? *(He reaches into his jacket pocket, pulls out a small recorder.)*

HEATHER You taped that? Excellent. Glad to hear it. Dumb-ass.

DOUG I'm not a dumb-ass. You're the dumb-ass, sister. Your dumb ass is grass. We're shutting this place down. Call in the undertaker, because the wrecking crew is here. *(Heather starts to giggle.)* I don't care if you respect the man, as long as you respect the badge.

HEATHER You should put on some pants.

A room at the police station, later that day. It has a table and chairs, and a telephone. There might be a two-way mirror. Sandy, in sweatpants and a sweatshirt, sits alone. Curt enters, carrying a file.

CURT Hi.

SANDY Hi. *(Curt consults the file.)*

CURT Sandy.

SANDY Yeah.

CURT Well, it's your lucky day, Sandy. I'm letting you go.

SANDY Really?

CURT Yep.

SANDY I don't have to pay a fine or anything?

CURT Nope. I should warn you, though, next time you won't get off so easy. You don't have a record. I'd like to see you keep it that way.

SANDY Yes sir.

CURT Before you go, would you mind answering a question?

SANDY Sure.

CURT Did you know I was a cop?

SANDY Yeah.

CURT How? *(Beat. She doesn't answer.)* Off the record.

SANDY You didn't take off your underwear.

CURT That was it?

SANDY That's how we know.

CURT Well, thanks for telling me.

(Doug enters.)

DOUG Can you believe this shit? I totally did not entrap that girl.

CURT I was just telling Sandy she could go.

SANDY *(To Doug.)* Say hi to your brother for me.

DOUG You know Scott?

SANDY Yeah. We were in band together.

DOUG No way. What's your name?

SANDY Sandy Waltham.

DOUG What'd you play?

SANDY Cymbals.

DOUG I thought you looked familiar! *(Indicating himself and Curt.)* We went to Hewitt.

SANDY I know. Well, see ya.

DOUG Hang on a minute. Not so fast. Okay? It's your lucky

day and you get to go home. But you might not've been so lucky. Did you think about that?

SANDY Yeah.

DOUG Do you know what Scott's doing right now?

SANDY Time?

DOUG That's so funny. You're so smart, aren't you? No. He's not doing time. Scott is an account executive for Wy-Tech in Omaha. He's got a great job and he's engaged to a great girl and he's doing great. I think of him, then I look at you and I think, you were in the same band. And what are you doing?

SANDY I'm a massage therapist.

DOUG Let's not beat around the bush. We know you're a hooker. We maybe can't prove it right now, but we know you're a ho. A lady of the night. A ho. Do you know what happens to girls like you, Sandy? It's not pretty. Last year, we found this girl—she was a party girl, lived in one of those party houses down in Brightville? We found her in a ditch one day, naked. She was so high she didn't even know where she was. *(Small beat.)* Now, Sandy, I hate thinking about that girl. Because it makes me look at you, and even though I don't want to, it makes me see you in a ditch someplace. Maybe high. Maybe naked. And I hate that. *(Beat. He stares at her a little too long.)* I hate thinking of you naked.

CURT Doug—

DOUG But, Sandy, I'm putting myself through this because I want to scare you. I want you to quit that job you're working at. I want you to take the brains and the talent that God gave you and go out there and get a good job—get a good job like Scott. Who is at Wy-Tech. In Omaha. Okay?

SANDY Okay.

DOUG Do you think I got through to you at all?

SANDY Yes.

DOUG Okay. I'll take that as a yes. *(He opens the door for her.)* Now, do you need a ride home?

SANDY Yeah.

DOUG Go over there—see Sergeant Michaels over there? *(Calls.)* Hey, Kenny! See if you can get this young lady a ride home. *(To Sandy)* Are we cool?

SANDY Yeah.

DOUG *(Gives her a thumbs up.)* Smokin'. We're cool. *(She*

walks off. He watches her for a second then closes the door. To Curt.) I think I made an impression.

CURT That was a really beautiful speech from somebody who just entirely fucked up our case.

DOUG Man. You know? She said she'd take a hundred.

CURT She said a hundred dollars could buy a lot of fun. She could have meant party hats. Balloons. A pony ride. A clown.

DOUG We'll just wait and in a couple of weeks we'll go back and we'll nail them.

CURT Oh, yeah, because they won't be expecting us now.

DOUG Why are you so mad at me?

CURT I put this thing together. We drilled and drilled, and in two minutes you fucked it up.

DOUG You didn't do any better.

CURT I didn't blow my cover!

DOUG She knew you were a cop. That's why she didn't have sex with you. So you can't say I tipped them off. They were already tipped off. *(Curt looks crushed.)* Look, you know, you haven't been working vice that long. You just gotta learn the ropes. Shit happens. No biggie.
Tomorrow's a new day. Right?

CURT I guess.

DOUG Okay. So here's what kills me. This whore is like, anal sex? No big deal. I couldn't believe it.

CURT That's how it works.

DOUG I just never had a girl let me fuck her up the ass before. Have you?

CURT I've never asked.

DOUG Well, me neither. I'm just saying, this is the first time a girl ever said she would.

CURT She's a hooker.

DOUG I don't know if I'd want to or not. I mean part of me is like, "Hell yeah, why the hell not?" But another part of me thinks it's kind of gay. Do you know what I mean? I mean, why not just fuck some guy up the ass?

CURT Are you through?

DOUG She said you could get a hand job for forty. But to me, paying a chick for a hand job is like totally admitting what a loser you are.

CURT I'm still wondering if you're through.

DOUG But that anal thing is definitely something to consider.

Scene Four

The kitchen of Curt's apartment, that night. It is very simple, almost spartan. He has a table and two chairs. His girlfriend, Beth, sits at the table flipping through magazines, looking at pictures and cutting out ones that strike her fancy. Curt makes himself something to eat.

CURT Two months down the fucking toilet. And he could care less. He wastes everybody's time, he totally blew it, and it's like there are no repercussions with him. He's oblivious.

BETH I don't see why you're still friends with him.

CURT We're not friends, really. We're just partners.

BETH He's such a jerk.

(Beat.)

CURT Could you not rag on my friends for once?

BETH So what's with this massage parlor? People don't like it?

CURT It's right next to the Ground Round. These Christian Coalition people take their kids there—you know they have this deal on Tuesday nights where they weigh your kid and you pay a penny a pound for their dinner? So all these families are pulling in the parking lot and their kids are like, "Mommy? Daddy? What's a massage parlor? What's adult entertainment? How can it be naughty *and* nice?" They're freaking out.

BETH That's what they get for going to the Ground Round.

CURT No, it's not. Just because they don't eat at . . . "La Paree" doesn't mean they deserve a whorehouse in the middle of Route Twenty-nine.

BETH "La Paree"?

CURT Or whatever those places are you like to eat.

BETH You mean places without drive-through windows?

CURT The Ground Round doesn't have a drive-through window.

BETH Okay then. Places that put something besides iceberg lettuce in the salads.

(Beat.)

CURT I like iceberg lettuce.

BETH *(Not hearing him. Overlapping.)* You know, you shouldn't close down this massage parlor, you should legalize it. These women aren't victims. They made a choice to be sex workers. If it was legal, they could

unionize and get health benefits. And safe working
conditions.

CURT *(Nods.)* Sounds good.

(Beat.)

BETH Don't do that.

CURT What?

BETH You're doing that thing where you think I'm full of
shit, but you just stand there and nod. Don't do that. If
you think I'm full of shit, tell me I'm full of shit.

CURT Okay. You're full of shit. You don't know the first
goddamn thing about it. Drive over to Malton Road some
night and see if these women look like they're in charge
of anything. They're pathetic. They can barely stand up.
They get the shit beat out of them on a regular basis and
every single last one of them is hooked on something
because it's just about the most demeaning thing you
could possibly do and the only way to feel better about it
is to be constantly stoned out of your fucking gourd.

(Beat.)

BETH Of course you know more about this than I do.

CURT On this particular subject, I do. Yes.

BETH Because you're worldly-wise.

CURT Because I'm a cop. You know? There's this one area
where I do happen to know more about some things than
you do.

BETH Fine.

CURT It's one very small area. But when I'm actually an
authority, I wish you'd just let me be the authority.

BETH Okay. You know more about hookers than I do.
Okay? Fine. Congratulations.

(Pause.)

CURT I don't know shit.

BETH (Laughs.) What?

CURT That's why I didn't catch that girl in the first place. I
went in there and I was like . . . (Shrugs.) I had no idea
what to do. I was like, "So, what's the oil for?" It was a
joke.

BETH Honey, you shouldn't feel bad that you didn't know
how to go to a hooker. That's a good thing.

CURT I know. I'm just mad at myself. I thought I was
prepared, but I got in there and all I could think was,
"Where do you do it?" There was just this table and one
chair. I guess you do it on the table, but it didn't seem
very stable. It seemed like it would collapse.

BETH Maybe you do it in the chair.

CURT It was a straight-back chair. Like that chair.

BETH You could do it in this chair. If you did it like a lap dance.

CURT I guess. And then—what do they do? Do they wash themselves out between guys?

BETH I don't know. I would think they probably douche or something. I don't know. *(Beat.)* Does each girl get her own room? Like, do they get to decorate their room?

CURT No. Nobody's assigned to a room, I don't think. There's this sort of big room when you come in. Like a conference room, almost. It's got this big round table and you go in, and the girls all come in and stand around the table, on the other side, then you pick out which one you want.

BETH You do?

CURT Yeah. It was weird. I was standing there looking at them, and they're all standing there in their underwear, right? Trying to look all sexy? And I looked at them and I realized that my number-one priority was cleanliness. Because I started thinking about what goes on in those rooms—

BETH We don't have to go into that.

CURT I know, think about it.

BETH *(Snaps.)* I don't want to.

(Beat.)

CURT You were the one just talking about douching and lap dances.

BETH But I don't want to talk about it anymore.

(Beat.)

CURT Okay. *(Pause. Curt eats. Beth closes a magazine.)*

BETH I gotta go.

CURT Why?

BETH I have all this material to get together before I leave tomorrow.

CURT I thought you were spending the night.

BETH I haven't even packed.

CURT I thought you were just driving to Monroe tomorrow.

BETH I am. But I have to get up early.

CURT Are you mad?

BETH No. I'm just tired.

CURT You're mad.

BETH I'm not. I'm just tired.

CURT Tired means mad.

BETH I'm not. Okay? I just want to spend the night in my own bed if that's okay. *(She gathers her things.)*

CURT When are you getting back?

BETH Sunday.

CURT Sunday?

BETH I'm doing a Friday–Saturday at the Friends school.

CURT Oh. *(Beat.)* I'm sorry I have such a disgusting job.

BETH You keep saying that but then you don't even try and find another one.

CURT Because I don't have a lot of options. What do you want me to do? Work at the Quick Trip? Go out to Rockwell and shovel slag?

BETH I didn't say that.

CURT If I wasn't doing this I'd be fucking . . . knee-deep in chicken blood at the Purina plant.

BETH I'm not telling you to get some dirtball job.

CURT I don't have a trust fund, Beth. I have a high-school diploma.

BETH You always call it a trust fund, but that's not what it is. My grandfather gave me those stocks when I was born. *(Beat.)*

CURT Did you hear what you just said?

BETH Look, it's not your job that's the problem. Okay? I

just didn't know you had to pick a girl out. At that place. I

thought they assigned you one or something, and when

you said that, it made me kind of jealous. I don't know. I

just didn't like thinking of you in a room with a bunch of

scuzzy girls.

CURT I wasn't turned on or anything. That's my whole

point.

BETH I know. I just saw it all of a sudden and it made me

mad. It wasn't even rational on my part. I just— I sort of

freaked out for a second. It's no big deal.

CURT It was work.

BETH I know.

CURT I can't even remember what she looked like.

Scene Five

A bar. A few tables and chairs, some beer lights and posters.
Streamers of plastic flags along the walls. Green Bay Packer
flags. There is a door to a back room. Bob Seger's "Against
the Wind" is coming from the back room but the front room
is quiet. Curt sits alone at the bar, nursing a beer. Heather
is behind the bar. She is extremely drunk and in mid-
conversation.

HEATHER I lost my job last week? Well, first I got arrested,
then I got fired. But I didn't do anything! That's the
fucked-up part. It was so unfair. If I walked up to you and
said I'd give you a thousand dollars to kill somebody's cat
or something, is that fair?

CURT That's entrapment.

HEATHER Exactly! Oh my God. Shooter on the house. *(She*
pours him a shot of DeKuyper's Green Apple Pucker.) I
only started working here yesterday but they don't keep
tabs on the liquor at all. You can totally drink for free.
The way I do it is, I just take one shot from every bottle.

Here. *(She picks up a bottle of Malibu, pours herself a shot, and downs it.)* What do you want?

CURT I'm fine. *(She drinks the DeKuyper's.)* Where's your boss?

HEATHER He's an old guy. He didn't like working late. He needed somebody to work nights. Did I tell you I lost my job? Well, first I got arrested— *(Sandy enters.)* Sandy!

SANDY Hey. *(To Curt.)* Hi.

CURT Hi. Do you want to sit here? Or go in the back?

SANDY This is fine. *(She sits.)*

HEATHER Is this the guy?

SANDY Yeah.

HEATHER *(She holds up her hand for a high five.)* High five, bro! *(Sandy and Curt look at each other, then Curt gives her a high five. To Sandy.)* I was telling him how I got arrested.

SANDY He knows.

HEATHER *(Delighted.)* How did you know?

SANDY He's a cop, Heather. He was one of the cops who arrested us. *(Heather stares at him, dumbfounded.)*

HEATHER You fucker! I can't believe I gave you a free

shooter! *(She grabs the bottle of Malibu. She turns and walks toward the back room.)* I am giving free shooters to these people back here who are NOT COPS! *(She exits. Beat.)*

CURT Well then.

SANDY Well.

CURT Thanks for coming.

SANDY Sure.

(Small beat.)

CURT Do you want a drink?

SANDY No thanks.

CURT Me neither, really.

SANDY We can just sit.

CURT Okay. I think maybe . . . do you want to shoot some pool?

SANDY I suck.

CURT Good then. I do too. *(Getting pool cues.)* It's good if you suck. It makes the games last longer.

SANDY Yeah. *(Curt puts quarters in the table, racks the balls, and so on; they begin to play throughout this.)*

CURT This is a nice place. That you picked out.

SANDY I didn't ever come here until last night. I'll probably come here as long as Heather's working.

CURT Are you two friends?

SANDY No. We're roommates.

CURT Really?

SANDY Just temporary. She got kicked out of her apartment. *(Beat.)* I almost didn't come. But then I wondered—I know you said I wasn't—but I wondered if I'd get in trouble if I didn't come.

CURT I promise, it's like I said. I just wanted to see you. Just as a guy. Not as a cop.

SANDY Okay. *(Beat.)* So you want a date?

CURT By date do you mean . . . are you soliciting?

SANDY No. I wondered if you were asking me out on a date.

CURT No. I have a girlfriend.

SANDY Oh. *(Beat.)* So what do you want?

CURT I don't know. I just . . . *(Stops playing. Takes a deep breath.)* I just wanted to help. I know you're not twenty-one, first of all. And you seem smart. And like a basically decent person. If what you said was true, and you've only been working at that place for three months, then maybe you're not attached to that? I don't know. I just thought maybe I could help you find something else to do.

SANDY That's okay. I like it there.

CURT God.

SANDY It's not that bad. The pay is good. It's really easy—

CURT It's easy?

SANDY Yeah. *(Beat.)* Look, the guys who come in, they're not really sexually active. You know? They don't have girlfriends or anything. They're kind of fat, or ugly. Usually they're really fat. And they just . . . I don't know how to put it. They come really fast.

CURT I think you know how to put it.

SANDY And most of them just want a hand job. It's like, ten minutes tops. Usually less. And then they hand me forty bucks. I get to keep twenty. So if I do four hand jobs in an hour, that's eighty bucks an hour.

CURT And you're not worried about AIDS or . . . ?

SANDY They have to wear a rubber. It's not like what your partner said. It's not all sick or anything. You just go in, you work your eight hours, and you go home.

CURT It's not right.

SANDY Look, no offense, okay? But I don't want to waste your time. You're not going to talk me out of it. I'm an adult. I've made a decision. This is what I want to do. I like it. So don't worry about it.

(Beat.)

CURT So do your parents know about this?

SANDY My mom doesn't, but Lucy does.

CURT Who's Lucy?

SANDY She's my mom's partner. Or wife or whatever you want to call it. Her lesbian life partner, I guess. Whatever. Lucy knows. But she doesn't care. She grew up in a really bad neighborhood, and she just says you gotta do what you gotta do. She's killed some people. In self-defense.

(Beat. He decides what part of that to tackle.)

CURT Your mom's a lesbian?

SANDY Yeah. Or so she says. I don't know. My mom's been married five times. Six if you count Lucy. That's sort of why I got into this, because Lucy moved in with all her kids. She has five kids. Two of them are gone, like dead or in jail or something, nobody knows. The last three all live

with her, even though they're way past twenty. And then
her daughter has a kid and he's there too. They just
moved in. One day I woke up and there were five new
people in the house. And my mom told me I'd have to
share my room with Denise and her kid. But Denise is,
like, a convicted drug dealer? She has one of those things
on her ankle? And she can't leave the house? She's just
always sitting in my room watching TV. And she doesn't
take care of her kid at all. I mean he smells bad. She
never gives him a bath. And nobody's paying rent, or
helping out with groceries. They're totally taking
advantage of us. I told my mom, I said, "You're such an
idiot. This is just like when you married Larry." Larry was
this guy she was married to for two weeks and he stole
all our money. We had a house over in Stanton and we
sold it and he stole all the money we got. Like twenty
thousand dollars, and we never got it back. So I just told
her, I said, "I'm sick of how stupid you are. I'm sick of my
whole life getting fucked up just because you can't stand
to be by yourself. I'm an adult, I'm moving out of the
house." *(Shrugs.)* She didn't even care. She just let
Denise have my room. Then she calls me up the other day

and asks me for a loan. I said, "Get a job. I'm not giving you money."

CURT What does she do?

SANDY She's a full-time alcoholic. When I graduated, I gave her my diploma and I said, "Here. You take this because you never graduated from high school so I want you to have it and hang it on the wall as a reminder of the one thing I did that you never did." And I just took my tassel and I hung it from the rearview mirror of my car and I said, "That's all I need. I'm hanging my tassel there because then I'll always have it in front of me when I'm driving, so it represents my goals and my dreams and I'll always have that in front of me while all you have is what's behind you, which is the big fucking wreck you made of your whole life."

(Beat.)

CURT My dad was a grave robber.

SANDY What?

CURT He worked on the grounds crew at a cemetery in Milwaukee, and he and the other guys, before they sealed up the graves, they would steal jewelry from the corpses. They got away with it for years, but then this man saw his dead wife's brooch in the window of a pawnshop. He had had it designed especially for her, with her name in rubies. The police figured it out right away. The whole grounds crew got busted. I was eleven. My mom didn't know about it. My dad spent all the money, I guess. She divorced him and we changed our names and we moved here.

SANDY Is that why you became a cop?

CURT No. I don't know why I became a cop.

SANDY I do what I do to make money. You at least ought to know why you do what you do.

CURT I do it to help people. I think. Like I want to help you.

SANDY Well. I appreciate it. But like I said, I don't need your help.

(*Heather comes in with the deliberateness of someone who is completely wasted. She goes behind the bar and takes out five shot glasses and lines them up on the bar. Then she takes two bottles and puts them next to the shot glasses. Then she turns her back on Curt and Sandy, pulls down her pants, and slaps her bare ass with each hand—slap, slap. Then she pulls up her pants, turns around, puts the five fingers of her right hand in each of the shot glasses,*

pulls them together, and picks them up. Then she picks up

the bottles with her left hand and very carefully walks back

into the back room. Beat.)

CURT Have you ever thought about going to college?

SANDY My grades sucked.

CURT My girlfriend is an artist. And she works with this
woman who's a professor over at Kirkwood? Community
College? I know they don't have as strict requirements
as a four-year school. Have you ever thought about
that?

SANDY I don't want to go to a community college. People
who go to community college are depressing.

CURT More depressing than prostitutes?

SANDY My cousin went to community college. And he took
this one design class, and he showed me his final project,
and basically all it was was a bunch of plastic triangles
glued together on this poster board. And he got an A on
it. And he's sitting there, telling me how he's going to be a
graphic designer. And I'm looking at him and I'm smiling,
and I'm saying, "That's great, Casey. That's great." But he

doesn't even know how to turn on a computer. He's not going to be a graphic designer. His teacher is lying to him.

CURT Maybe not.

SANDY Gluing triangles together is not designing graphics. I mean, haven't you ever looked at somebody and said, "That's great"? But inside of you, you know that it's never going to happen? *(Beat. He doesn't answer.)* See?

CURT So what is it you want to do?

SANDY I want to do what I'm doing.

CURT These are the hopes and dreams you keep in front of you?

SANDY I don't know what I want to do. Okay? I just know what I *don't* want to do, and I don't want to do that. I don't want to go to community college and learn how to type and go be a word processor someplace or do data entry or food service or any of that crap. Nobody actually *wants* to do any of those things. *(Beat.)* A guy comes in, and not to be crude, but he puts it in and he comes. And I'm like, "That was it?" And then he hands me a hundred bucks, and I'm looking at the clock going, "Excellent." *(It hits her.)* I tell you what, if there's anything I want, I want to keep the whole hundred instead of giving half to the house.

(Pause.)

CURT Well, if I can't help you, maybe you could help me.

(Sighs.) There is this one thing my girlfriend won't do.

Curt's kitchen, later that night. Sandy has a stack of pressed leaves in plastic and two sheets of paper. She is shuffling the leaves. Curt is getting them two beers.

SANDY *(Finishes shuffling.)* Okay. I'm ready.

CURT Excellent. You got the key—that's for this set.

SANDY I got it. *(They sit across from each other at the table.)*

CURT Okay. Shoot. *(Sandy holds up a leaf. Each leaf has a number on the corner of the plastic, which Sandy checks against a key.)* Burr oak.

SANDY Yes. *(She holds up another.)*

CURT Osage orange.

SANDY Yes. *(Another.)*

CURT Honey locust.

SANDY Yep. *(Starts to hold up another one, stops.)* Why wouldn't your girlfriend do this?

CURT Well, it's not really fair to say she wouldn't do it. She was willing to do it, but it was just too complicated. She has, like, a number-lexia. She can read fine, but she transposes numbers? *(Sandy stares at him.)* For some reason she couldn't match the numbers to the key. So I came in with my first hundred, and I thought I had them down pretty good, but I was missing every single one. And I was getting so pissed. And then I realized, after about an hour of this, that I was getting them right but she was reading the fucking key wrong. I lost it. Beth started crying. It was ugly. So it seemed like I better do it myself. But it's hard to do by yourself.

SANDY I bet. *(Holds up another one.)*

CURT Silver maple.

SANDY Your girlfriend's an artist?

CURT She does the artists-in-the-school program.

SANDY What's that?

CURT She goes around the state. She teaches art at different schools. Or something.

SANDY You don't know?

CURT I . . . *(Beat.)* I shouldn't talk about Beth.

SANDY Sorry.

CURT No, it's okay. I just—we—

SANDY You don't have to say anything.

CURT We're getting married.

SANDY Oh. I didn't know that.

CURT We come from different backgrounds. Is all I was
going to say. Which is good.

SANDY Sure. *(Holds up another.)*

CURT Bigtooth aspen. *(Another.)* Chinquapin oak.

SANDY I like these names.

CURT Aren't they nice?

SANDY They're pretty.

CURT Do you ever go up to the preserve?

SANDY No. I mean, I think I went once when I was a kid.
My third stepdad was a big-time hunter and I think we
drove up there once and picked him up when he was too
drunk to drive home.

(Beat.)

CURT Well, it's really nice, if you ever want to go up there.
The nature center has this really cool bird-viewing room.
The glass is a two-way mirror, so the birds see their own
reflections and you don't scare them off. They put bird
feeders right next to the window so you can see the birds
really close. It's so cool. If I have a house someday, I want
to do that.

SANDY Maybe I'll check it out.

CURT *(Embarrassed by his enthusiasm.)* You don't have to.

SANDY No. It sounds nice. I will. *(Holds up a leaf.)*

CURT Quaking aspen. *(Another.)* Hackberry. *(Another.)* Aaah, don't tell me. Chokecherry.

SANDY Kentucky coffee tree.

CURT Fuck. *(He takes it from her to study.)*

SANDY So you want to work at this nature center?

CURT I guess, what I want, is to be a volunteer guide. But I talked to the ranger, and they won't take just anybody. A lot of the guys who do it now are retired teachers and they don't want to give up their slots. Because it's so cool, you know? I think, anyway.

SANDY It sounds cool. It sounds like— I don't know. The air would smell good.

CURT It does. So I figure if I learn these now, then when I retire, maybe I can be a guide.

SANDY That's good. To have something to look forward to.

CURT Yeah. *(Small beat.)* Give me another one. *(She holds one up.)* Shagbark hickory. The thing is, if I could've gone to college, I think I probably would've studied forestry or something like that. Then I would have gotten a job with the DNR. But it didn't work out that way.

SANDY How come?

CURT My mom was sick for a long time and I had to take care of her. She died last year.

SANDY I'm sorry.

CURT Thanks. *(She holds up another.)*

SANDY Have you ever shot anybody?

CURT No. *(Curt stares at the leaf, then at her. Beat.)* I don't usually talk so much.

SANDY It's okay. I like this. *(Pause. They look at each other.)*

CURT You have really pretty hands.

SANDY Thanks.

CURT I could tell you had soft skin. When you gave me the massage.

SANDY Your back's real strong. *(Beat.)* Muscular.

(Pause. They look at each other, they might kiss, but don't. They look away.)

CURT Why do you think you want some things?

SANDY I don't know.

CURT I think about that a lot. Why you want what you

want. I don't think very many of us know what we're

doing.

(Beat.)

SANDY You want to keep going?

CURT Yeah. *(She holds up a leaf.)* I mean, I'm doing really

good. For somebody from my background, this is really

good, what I'm doing. Being a detective. But even then,

some days I feel like I'm just banging my head against a

wall. *(Motions toward the leaf.)* I have to sit here and

teach myself what all the trees are. You know? *(Beat. He*

is lost in thought, troubled. Then he snaps out of it.

Indicating the leaf.) American plum.

SANDY *(Finished.)* That's it.

CURT That's it? Really?

SANDY That's the first set. You did good.

CURT You want to do another set?

SANDY I'm kind of tired.

CURT Oh.

SANDY It's two in the morning.

CURT Right.

SANDY I had a good time, though.

CURT Me too.

(Beat.)

SANDY You know, if you wanted to ask me to do it again, like, next Friday night? I'd probably say yes.

CURT (Quickly.) Do you want to do this again next Friday night?

SANDY (Quickly.) Yes.

(Beat. Curt smiles.)

CURT All right then.

Scene Seven

The room at the police station, a week later. Doug is asleep on the table, curled up in a fetal position, his head on his wadded-up jacket. Curt enters, turns on the lights. Doug sits up quickly. Curt carries a newspaper.

DOUG Oh man. Is it time for the meeting?

CURT It's over.

DOUG Come on. Let's go.

CURT The meeting's over. The meeting was at two.

DOUG *(Looks at his watch.)* Shit. Did you cover for me?

CURT No.

DOUG Oh well. What are you gonna do? Right? *(Curt doesn't answer.)* So what's the deal, anyway?

CURT Oh. It was just about this newspaper article. *(He hands the paper to Doug, who stares at it blankly.)* There on the front page. *(Takes it back.)* Let me help you out there. Let's start with the picture. See these nice people in the sweaters and the suits, standing outside the Naughty But Nice massage parlor? They're mad. That's why they're holding these signs. The signs say,

"Concerned Citizens Coalition. Clean up our city. Save our children." See this minister right here? He's super-mad. He wants the place shut down. He says the mayor is ignoring their pleas. But the mayor is saying it's not his fault, it's the cops'. That the cops made an arrest but they botched it. So they had to throw the whole case out on a stupid technicality.

DOUG Is the lieutenant mad?

CURT Gosh, let's see. He took us off the case. He put me back on the fucking burglary unit.

DOUG Man. So who'd he put in charge of this?

CURT Bill Horton. He told me I don't know when to ask for help.

DOUG Who did?

CURT The lieutenant. *(Beat.)* I was so glad when they took me off burglary. I can't tell you how much I hated burglary.

DOUG Well, the joke's on Bill Horton because there's no way they're gonna catch them now. The girls aren't taking any new customers. If they don't know you, no luck.

CURT How do you know that?

DOUG I heard.

CURT Who from?

DOUG People. *(Curt studies him.)* Nobody.

CURT If you went back in there, I'll kill you.

DOUG I didn't. I swear.

CURT Then what?

DOUG I've kind of been hanging out with that one girl. The
girl I went to. But she doesn't work there anymore. So it's
fine.

CURT Heather?

DOUG Yeah. We've kind of been, you know, dating. But her
roommate is that Sandy? She still works there and that's
what she said. That they're totally suspicious. They're
even frisking guys.

CURT Back up. When did she say this?

DOUG I don't know. The other night. I've been kind of
hanging out at their house. That was the funny thing. I
couldn't find Heather at first, because the number in her
file was disconnected, so I called Sandy and it turns out
they're living together. So Heather was like, "Yeah, come
down and meet me after work." I didn't know what I was
going to do. 'Cause I didn't know, was it gonna be free,
would I have to pay? But it turns out she's just this really

sweet girl and she just wants to have a good time and so
we're dating. I mean, I'm not paying her or anything.

CURT That's good. Because that's really all I was worried
about. I just want to make sure you're having sex for free.

DOUG I'm only telling you this because you're doing it too.

CURT What?

DOUG With Sandy. You better be careful, though. You're
engaged.

CURT Who said that? Sandy?

DOUG Not in so many words. But you know, she intimated.

CURT What did she say?

DOUG She said you two got back to nature.

CURT When was this?

DOUG Last night at her house. They were having a party. No
surprise, though. It's a total party house. That's why I fell
asleep. I hadn't been getting any sleep. But what did you
do? I didn't get it.

CURT We didn't do anything. Did she mention— She's
supposed to come over again this Friday. Did she say
anything about that?

DOUG Nope. She wasn't in the mood for talking. She was
getting wild. She kept walking around, making people

shake her hand. She wanted to know if her hand felt like a pussy. A couple of guys said, "Most definitely." You know? This one guy said, "There's only one way to know for sure." *(Laughs.)*

CURT Who are these guys?

DOUG I don't know. There's always a bunch of hosers over there. They follow Heather home from the bar. Here's the thing, though. I want to ask your advice on this. You know, there was that one thing about Heather that I was interested in. Which you know what that was. But the thing is, she won't do it. She said that was something she did for money, but it's not like she likes doing it, so she won't do it. So I was discussing this with Sandy last night, and I was saying, Heather's my girlfriend now, I need to respect her and all, but there's this thing I'm still interested in only she won't do it. And Sandy said, you know, *she'd* be willing to do it if I wanted. And I don't know, I don't want to cheat on Heather, but I got a hard-on just thinking about it— *(Curt punches him hard in the mouth. He staggers.)* Fuck! That hurt!

CURT *(Overlapping.)* Why do you act like that? You fucking idiot! *(Picks up the newspaper and hits him*

with every word.) You stupid, stupid fuck! You're ruining
my life!

DOUG *(Overlapping.)* Stop it!

CURT *(Jabbing his finger at the picture in the paper.)* See
these people? They're never gonna let up! They're never
gonna let up, and I'm the one who'll pay! I'll always pay
because I'm stuck with shit like you!

DOUG Shut up!

CURT *(Hitting Doug with the paper again.)* Stupid shit!

DOUG *(Doug is crying.)* I'm not stupid! I'm a detective on
the police force! I got— I made that! I made that! I made
that and I— That's what *I* did!

CURT You're ruining my life!

DOUG I am not ruining your life! Your life is not ruined!
Your life is so good! I would kill for your life! *(Small
beat.)* It's good. *(Pause. Doug wipes his nose and mouth
on his sleeve.)*

CURT Shit. *(Small beat.)* Your mouth is bleeding.

DOUG I'm sick of people telling me I can't do things.

CURT Let me look at your mouth.

DOUG I'm sick of it.

CURT God. I hit you in the mouth.

DOUG It's not fair.

CURT I'm sorry I hit you.

DOUG Fuck. *(They stand for a moment.)* I'm crying like a fucking girl.

CURT I'm sorry.

(Not looking at each other.)

DOUG Your life is good.

Curt's apartment. Night. Someone is knocking on the back door. It's not hugely loud, but it's persistent. Curt comes in in a T-shirt and sweatpants, half asleep. He goes to the door, turns on the outside light, and looks through the curtain. He opens the door. Sandy is standing there, barefoot, no coat. She's been crying.

SANDY I'm sorry. I'm sorry I woke you up.

CURT What do you want?

SANDY I can't stay at my apartment. There're all these people at my apartment and I couldn't get them to leave. I was screaming and crying and I couldn't get them to leave. It's totally out of control.

CURT Come on in. Do you want me to call somebody?

SANDY Your stupid friend is there. He wouldn't do anything.

CURT Why aren't you wearing shoes? It's freezing outside.

(He sits her down, hands her a dish towel.)

SANDY I told Heather she had to have everybody out by tonight or I was kicking her out. Then I came home and there were like fifty people there and I don't know any of them.

CURT Keep talking. I'm listening. *(He exits.)*

SANDY *(Toweling off her feet.)* I was so tired and all I wanted to do was go to sleep but I went in my room, and these people I didn't even know were sitting on my bed snorting cocaine off my dresser mirror. I have this dresser set my grandmother gave me before she died, and they took the mirror off the wall and they're snorting cocaine off it.

CURT *(Enters with socks.)* Put these on.

SANDY *(Breathes, trying not to cry. Puts on the socks.)* Every time I try and have something nice it just gets totally ruined. I don't have any nice clothes. I don't have any nice furniture. I have one nice thing my grandmother gave me and now it's ruined. *(Beat.)* God. I'm sorry. I didn't know where else to go. I didn't come by on Friday.

CURT I know.

SANDY Doug told me that you hit him.

CURT Yeah.

SANDY I was drunk. When I said that stuff to him. I don't even remember what I said. I came home and I sat down and I got drunk. My last stepdad died. He's the only one I ever liked and he died on Tuesday from lung cancer. He was at the V.A. hospital for six months and I never even went to see him. My mom just left me a message on my machine. "Roy died." So I just sat down and got drunk and then I let some guy I didn't even know go to bed with me. It was disgusting. But I would have done it anyway. Even if my stepdad hadn't died, I would have found some other reason.

CURT Why?

SANDY Because. I'm just so fucked up. *(She starts crying again.)* God. *(She wipes her nose on the dish towel.)*

CURT Don't use that. *(He gets a fresh towel from the drawer.)* You wiped your feet on it.

SANDY I can't believe how nice you are to me. Why are you so nice to me?

CURT I don't know.

SANDY I'm such an idiot. I like you so much. But I couldn't come back here on Friday. I just had been so gross all week and I couldn't come back here because I knew you would know.

CURT I put too much pressure on you. I know . . . people

have their ways—

SANDY Don't think that!

CURT I'm thirty-six years old. I never should have even

talked to you.

SANDY Why?

CURT It's not right. I just felt like we had something in

common—

SANDY We do.

CURT But I shouldn't have expected so much from you.

(Beat. She's stricken.)

SANDY That's the meanest thing anybody's ever said to me!

God! *(She gets up, heads for the door.)*

CURT Hang on! Where are you going?

SANDY Someplace else!

CURT Sandy, wait. You're gonna have a wreck. Just sit here

and calm down for a second. Okay? *(She sits.)* I'm just

saying, you never said you'd quit or anything. I just—in

my head, I just had this idea that you would. Because, I

had this stupid idea that—that things could be different.

For you. I don't know for me. But for you. *(Beat.)* I don't know what I was thinking. I don't know. I spent all week wondering what the hell I was doing with you and I still don't know.

(Pause.)

SANDY Before, you said you wanted to help me—

CURT I don't know what I wanted.

SANDY If you wanted to help me, though, if you still want to—I guess—I think I could really use your help.

(Long pause. Curt doesn't look at her for a long time, and then he nods, almost to himself.)

CURT Do you want to spend the night?

SANDY Yeah.

CURT Okay then. You can spend the night.

(Sandy nods. She gets up, hands Curt the dish towel, and heads into the living room. Curt waits until she's passed through the door, then turns off the kitchen light.)

act two

Curt's kitchen, two days later. Sandy and Curt are sitting at the kitchen table. Sandy is cleaned up. She wears a pair of Curt's sweatpants and one of his shirts. Curt is in sweatpants and a T-shirt too. They are sipping coffee and reading the want ads. Duke Ellington's "Blue Serge" is playing in the next room.

SANDY Just— I don't want food service. If I have to work at Wendy's, I'll quit after one day. *(Curt looks at her.)* I'm just being honest.

CURT But retail is okay?

SANDY I can do retail if I have to. *(They go back to the paper. Beat.)* I like this song.

CURT Yeah. Beth's really into jazz, and when we first started dating she'd play me all these CDs. I liked this one. She said, "It's Duke Ellington. 'Blue Serge.' " And I thought, "Yeah. Exactly." Because I could see it. You know? This surge of blueness coming out of the song. Like a sadness.

SANDY Yeah.

CURT Then the next time we were listening to the CD, I
told Beth how I saw this surge of sadness in the song and
that's when she told me it was really about a cheap suit.

SANDY What?

CURT It's "Blue Serge." S-e-r-g-e. Like a blue serge suit?
(Sandy shakes her head.) I guess it's a material. Like a
cheap cotton or something.

SANDY Never heard of it.

CURT Me neither.

SANDY *(Listens.)* It's still a sad song, though.

CURT Yeah.

SANDY I would definitely think what you thought. *(Beat.)*
Maybe it's about a guy who's sad because all he can
afford is a cheap suit.

CURT Maybe.

SANDY That would make me sad. *(Beat.)* At my graduation,
you had to wear a dress under your gown. And I saved up
and bought this red dress? I thought it looked really good.
It even had a belt that came with it. But when I got there,
like all the other girls had on these super nice dresses
and all of a sudden I was looking at mine, and it was like,
the belt didn't look like leather anymore. It looked like

plastic. *(Pause.)* I don't know. My nicest thing was not even anywhere near as nice as their cruddiest thing.

CURT When I was a kid, I could never have anybody over to my house because my mom was sick all the time. She was so depressed she just never got off the couch basically. But she had five dogs and she couldn't get off her ass to let them outside. She'd just let them go down in the basement. In the winter she'd crank up the heat, I'd come home from school, open the door . . . roasted shit.

SANDY Gross.

(They're laughing. A jangling of keys at the door. They both look up. Beth enters with an overnight bag.)

CURT Hey. *(He gets up to take her bag. She looks at Sandy.)*

BETH Hi.

CURT You made good time.

BETH Yeah.

CURT This is Sandy.

BETH Uh-huh.

CURT Sandy, this is Beth.

SANDY Hey. I've heard a lot about you.

BETH Uh-huh.

CURT How was the trip?

BETH *(Still staring at Sandy.)* Fine.

CURT Good. *(Beat.)* Sandy needed a place to stay so I let her sleep on the couch for a couple of nights.

BETH I don't know about Sandy, do I?

CURT No. Um . . . no. You know, you've been in and out of town so much, I didn't really have a chance to tell you. But I met Sandy, I guess three or four weeks ago . . . ? *(He turns to Sandy.)*

SANDY Three weeks ago. His partner is dating my roommate.

BETH Oh.

CURT Doug is dating her roommate.

SANDY Yeah. And they keep partying at my house. So. *(Small beat.)* I couldn't get any sleep and Curt said I could stay here. But I'm going now.

CURT No.

SANDY I should go. I'll just get dressed.

CURT Where are you gonna go?

SANDY Back to my place.

CURT You can't go back there.

SANDY It's fine. I'll just get dressed. *(She exits.)*

CURT *(Following her.)* Sandy, you can't go back there—

BETH Curt!

CURT *(Stops.)* What?

BETH What the hell's going on?

CURT Nothing.

BETH Do you have some woman over here every time I go out of town?

CURT No. I just met her and she needed a place to stay. She came over here, it was raining outside, she didn't even have any shoes on—

BETH Why did she come over here?

CURT She didn't have any place else to go.

BETH How did she know to come over here, though? She's been here before?

CURT Just once.

BETH When?

CURT When you were in Monroe. A couple of weeks ago. She came over here and helped me with my leaves.

BETH What?

CURT She was helping me learn my leaves.

BETH This seems really wrong.

CURT I'm not cheating on you. Okay? Just sit tight. *(He exits.)*

BETH Curt! *(Beat. She exits into the living room. Off.)* Where are you going? *(Beat. Farther off.)* What the hell are you doing?

CURT *(Off.)* We're talking.

BETH *(Off.)* What's going on!

CURT *(Off.)* Nothing!

SANDY *(Off. Coming closer.)* I don't want to start a fight.

CURT *(Off.)* Just sit down and talk then.

SANDY *(Entering in her pants and a bra, carrying her shirt. Curt and Beth follow.)* I should just go, because I'm making you guys fight.

CURT I don't want you to go back there.

SANDY Everybody's prob'ly passed out by now anyway.

CURT You don't even have any shoes. Sit down and let's talk.

BETH Why don't you let her put her shirt on.

SANDY See? I'm just messing everything up. This is what I do. I mess things up.

CURT What are you going to do?

SANDY It's not your problem. *(She exits.)*

CURT *(Exiting behind her.)* Sandy! Don't go if you don't know where you're going!

SANDY *(Off.)* You better go inside, because your girlfriend is mad at you.

CURT *(Off.)* Sandy!

SANDY *(Off.)* Now you're not wearing shoes. *(Pause. Beth stands at the door, waiting. Curt comes back inside, closes the door behind him. They stare at each other.)*

BETH You want to tell me what's going on?

CURT I better go after her. *(He starts putting on his shoes.)*

BETH Why? What is going on?

CURT She's somebody I wanted to help. That's all. I met her. I wanted to help.

BETH Where did you meet her? *(He doesn't answer.)* Curt?

CURT At that massage parlor.

BETH Is that that prostitute?

CURT Yes.

BETH Yes!

CURT Look, Beth, I'm sorry. I should've told you, but—

BETH *(Overlapping.)* What did you do?

CURT I didn't do anything!

BETH Why don't I believe you?

CURT I didn't do anything!

BETH But you wanted to, didn't you? *(Pause.)* Did you want to?

CURT I can't do this right now. I have to go after her.

BETH She's some whore, you're going after some whore instead of staying here and talking to me? I need you to stay here and talk to me!

CURT I can't. *(He gets his car keys and wallet. As he does:)*

BETH Then don't you expect me to stand here and wait for you. If you go after her, don't you fucking expect to see me again!

CURT Maybe you'll understand this someday or maybe you won't but I have to go.

(He exits. Beth looks after him, crushed.)

BETH Well, that answers my question, doesn't it.

The bar, that night. Heather is tending bar, Doug is at the bar.

DOUG We gotta get our tickets early. So we need to commit now if we want to go.

HEATHER I don't want to sleep on the ground.

DOUG We won't. I got an air mattress, I'll put it in the back of the truck. We'll look up at the stars. It'll be nice.

HEATHER Who's playing?

DOUG Styx. Doobie Brothers. Creedence Clearwater Revisited.

HEATHER A bunch of old farts, playing out in some field? That sounds kind of sucky to me.

DOUG It's three days of classic rock.

HEATHER Where do people pee?

(Curt enters, upset.)

DOUG Hey man! You want to go to Rockfest this summer?

CURT Have you guys seen Sandy?

HEATHER Not since Friday.

DOUG We thought she was with you.

CURT What's the deal with your apartment?

HEATHER What?

CURT There's an eviction notice and a padlock on the door.

HEATHER No way! When?

CURT This morning. I went by this morning. Do you know where Sandy's mom lives?

HEATHER *(Picking up the phone.)* That's such bullshit! We paid the rent. *(Dials.)*

DOUG She left before we did, but we figured she'd be back.

CURT When did you leave?

DOUG I don't know. *(To Heather.)* When did we leave?

HEATHER *(Into phone.)* It's me, are you there?

DOUG *(To Curt.)* We had to get some sleep so we went back to my place.

HEATHER *(Into phone.)* Pick up the fucking phone, Sandy.

CURT So people were still at this party?

DOUG Man, it was insane. We figured Sandy'd be back, though. You know. No harm.

HEATHER Sandy? *(Hangs up.)* Where the fuck is she?

CURT That's what I'm trying to find out. Do you know where her mom lives?

HEATHER No. Did you try her at work?

CURT She wouldn't be there.

HEATHER I think she was supposed to work today.

CURT No.

HEATHER They can't put a padlock on my door. My stuff is in there.

DOUG Legally speaking—

HEATHER Shut up. *(Sandy enters.)* Hey! What the hell's going on?

SANDY I had to give the fucking landlord five hundred dollars before he'd let me back in the apartment! He put a big padlock on the door. What'd you do?

HEATHER I didn't do anything!

CURT *(Overlapping.)* Where have you been?

SANDY *(To Curt.)* I went to my mom's house and she told me I couldn't stay there so I went back home and there's this padlock— I couldn't even get in the door and I'm standing there, and the landlord comes around the corner screaming his head off at me— He couldn't find me and he kicked everybody out and he said the place is trashed. What did you do?

HEATHER I didn't do anything! I wasn't even there!

DOUG We had to get some sleep.

SANDY You just left my apartment with all these people in it?

HEATHER Well, where the fuck were you? I haven't seen you in two days. Shacked up with some fucking cop—

DOUG Hey.

HEATHER Seriously, though. Why is your apartment my responsibility?

SANDY Because you live there!

CURT *(To Sandy.)* Where have you been this whole time?

SANDY I went to work.

CURT You went to work?

SANDY I had to get five hundred bucks to pay the fucking landlord! *(To Heather.)* Give me the key!

HEATHER No way!

SANDY Give me the key right now!

HEATHER I'm getting my stuff. You can't keep my stuff!

SANDY You owe me five hundred bucks. Give me five hundred bucks you can get your stuff!

CURT *(Bangs his hand on the bar, very loud.)* Shut up about the money! *(Beat. They're all quiet. To Sandy.)* You went back to work?

SANDY What else was I supposed to do?

CURT Call me? *(Sandy stares at him.)* Pick up the phone
and call me?

SANDY I didn't think of it.

CURT What?

SANDY I couldn't get in my apartment. *(Curt stares at her.)*
I'm sorry. Your girlfriend was mad.

CURT How did you do it?

SANDY What?

CURT Five hundred dollars. How did you do it? *(Beat.)*

SANDY *(Quiet.)* I worked all day.

CURT I spent all day in the car. All day driving around—I
didn't know where you were—I tried to find your mom in
the phone book—

SANDY She goes by my second dad's name—

CURT I thought maybe the Super America, maybe the
Laundromat? I didn't know! I didn't know. But the one
place I did not look because we had agreed—! We had
agreed that you would not go back there—

SANDY *(Overlapping.)* I didn't know what else to do!

CURT I did not once drive out Route Twenty-nine and I did
not once think of looking in there because I did not once
think you would be stupid enough to go back there!

SANDY *(Quiet.)* I didn't have a coat.

CURT You didn't have a coat?! What the—! Put it together, Sandy. You didn't have a coat so you go whore like some fucking skank piece of trash?

SANDY Curt.

CURT What is in your head? Is there anything in your head or are you just one giant cunt—

HEATHER Hey—

CURT Just a fucking cunt that I fucking drove all over town— I left my fiancée standing there thinking I had slept with you, like I would come near you, you're a fucking petri dish—

SANDY I couldn't get in my apartment, I didn't have a coat, I didn't know what else to do!

CURT Well, I guess, you know, your resolve lasted a couple of hours at least. I guess that's something, isn't it. That's something right there. *(He exits.)*

SANDY Fine then. You know? Fuck you. You tell me what I should've done now but you weren't there and you don't know!

HEATHER Exactly.

SANDY God. Would you shut up? You're such a fucking whore!

HEATHER I'm getting my stuff tonight.

SANDY Fine. Fuck everybody.

(She exits. Beat.)

HEATHER Now I have to find someplace else to live. *(To Doug.)* Let me move in with you. *(Doug looks surprised. Thinks.)*

DOUG On one condition.

HEATHER Fine. All right? We can have anal sex.

DOUG Wow, really?

HEATHER Yes.

DOUG Excellent! Thank you.

HEATHER God.

DOUG That wasn't the condition, though.

HEATHER What?

DOUG I just wanted to go to Rockfest.

A few hours later. Curt's kitchen. It is dark. He sits at the kitchen table, drinking beer. It is silent. A jangling of keys. Beth enters, turns on the light. Jumps.

BETH God. *(Small beat.)* You're sitting here in the dark? *(Curt doesn't answer.)* I needed to get something. I came over to get something.

CURT What?

BETH Nothing. I was going to wait for you. *(Beat.)* I thought we should talk. *(Beat.)* Where's your car?

CURT I ran out of gas.

BETH Where'd you run out of gas?

CURT Down the street. The gauge is broken. I keep track by the miles but I wasn't looking at the odometer. But you know that.

BETH Where have you been?

CURT Driving around. I drove by your house.

BETH Why didn't you come in?

CURT I figured you probably never wanted to talk to me again.

BETH The thought occurred to me.

CURT I've been an ass.

BETH You've been something.

CURT I'm an idiot.

BETH Did you sleep with that girl?

CURT I told you already. You're either going to believe me
or you're not.

(Beat.)

BETH It's just I can tell something went on. I just don't
know what.

CURT We just talked.

BETH And?

CURT I liked talking to her. I felt really comfortable around
her. We didn't fight. I'm always fighting with you.

BETH So . . . you like her more than me?

CURT No. I don't know. I just— It was nice, for a change, to
be able to talk about things I can't talk about with you.

BETH Like what?

CURT Like, things about my past and stuff.

BETH What, exactly?

CURT Things about, how it was when I was a kid. Things
you don't want to know. They're gross to you.

ıld you give me an example?

t things I don't think you'd understand. Because
you're rich.

BETH I'm not rich.

CURT Yes you are.

BETH No I'm not.

CURT Your family is rich.

BETH No they're not.

CURT Yes they are. *(Beat.)* They have rooms in their house
they don't even use.

BETH That's your standard?

CURT Yes.

BETH Well, *I'm* not rich.

CURT You don't make much money but you're rich. I mean
sure, you're broke—

BETH Exactly. I'm broke.

CURT But you're an artist. Money's not important to you.
But that's what you chose. A lot of people don't get to
choose. It's not an option for them. They're just fucked.
From day one. They're fucked. *(Laughs.)* In some cases,
literally.

BETH But do I treat you like . . . I mean, am I acting insensitive or something? I've never thought of myself as a snob or something—

CURT Not really, I guess. I mean, I don't think you know it when you do it. It's not like you're openly down on poor people. It's just that, you know, you don't know what you're talking about when you talk about them. You talk about them like they're all noble or something. Instead of just sad. Or what they are which is just . . . well me, first of all. I mean, I'm poor. I've always been poor. But also just whatever they are. Like half the time they're fine, and half the time they're shooting each other and screaming at each other and it's just embarrassing. I can see why people think they're a bunch of animals—

BETH I don't—

CURT *(Continuing.)* Which of course they're not. They're not animals. That's not true. But after a while, you do start to feel like maybe everybody's living in a cage. Everybody who's poor. Like maybe, every day you go to work but every night you just go back to your cage. You turn the lock. You go inside. You turn the lock again. And you sit. In your cage. And all you can hope for is one day, if you work hard enough, maybe you can score yourself a bigger cage. *(Looks around.)*

BETH You don't live in a cage—

CURT *(Overlapping.)* But that's how I feel. When I'm around you. I feel like you pity me, maybe. For not being able to get out of my cage.

BETH I never pitied you. I love you.

CURT I'm glad you think that but I don't always think that.

BETH How can you not think that?

CURT I think sometimes I'm a cop that you met at a bar. And you're marrying me because you're still looking for some way to shock your friends. Because who would ever think you'd marry some jackass cop? I mean, what could be more shocking than marrying a guy who was raised by wolves?

BETH You're not some sort of statement. You're who I want to marry.

CURT Even though I was raised by wolves? Insane wolves?

BETH I don't know what you mean by that.

CURT I mean, I don't know how to act. I don't know how to

be around people. I was so surprised when you said you'd go out with me. I couldn't believe it. I just freaked, basically. I figured I better not fuck up because I'd never have another chance like this. And for four years I've been sitting around, trying not to fuck up. Trying not to say the wrong thing. Trying not to let anybody know that, growing up, a big dinner at my house was deviled ham and crackers.

BETH You're exaggerating.

CURT No I'm not.

BETH *(Beat.)* Well then, so what?

CURT So what?

BETH Say it's true—

CURT It is true.

BETH Then what's your point?

CURT A big dinner at my house was deviled ham and crackers. Is my point.

BETH Do you want me to feel sorry for you? Because you're doing a pretty good job of that yourself.

CURT Thanks.

BETH No, I'm just— I'm sorry you had such a shitty

childhood. I wish I could change it, but I can't and it's in the past. And it's not an issue with me. Is my point.

CURT So I should get over it.

BETH Not get over it, but you can move past it, I think.

CURT Do you think that's maybe easier for you to say. Because it's not an issue for you?

(Beat.)

BETH Okay. My parents were definitely middle class—

CURT Rich.

BETH Upper middle class but that doesn't mean I don't understand what you're talking about, or that I don't care. I do care. But it's just where you come from, you know? It's not who you are.

CURT That's a nice sentiment. *(Beat.)* My point is this, though. I get this nervous sweat. Around you. And it smells bad. That's why I shower so much. Did you ever notice I shower a lot?

BETH You're kind of compulsive about it. Yeah.

CURT Did you ever wonder why?

BETH I just thought . . . maybe you run a lot. At work.

CURT I've walked around for four years afraid that you

think I stink. And I think a psychiatrist would tell me that that points to something in our relationship that maybe needs to be addressed.

BETH Then I would say he was right—

CURT *(Overlapping.)* Which is the fact that no matter how hard I try, I am never going to be as good as you—

BETH That's not true.

CURT Because you are never going to let me because you're rich. You're rich and rich people are always right and they're always better. Even if they decide to fucking marry you—they are always going to be right and you are always going to be wrong because rich people are good and poor people are bad.

BETH That's such bullshit.

CURT No, I know. Don't think I don't know. That's why I fucking hate the burglary unit. I spend all my time going over to the houses of rich people and something's gone, something's missing, and who knows what the fuck it is because they have so much fucking stuff to begin with. But whatever it is, it's gone. And it's a great big tragedy and I'm supposed to fix it. Like I'm some servant they called in. And I'm standing there thinking, "Some tragedy—just call your goddamn insurance agent." And then I feel it. The way I feel around rich people. It's the same way I feel around you. Like I'm stupid and I stink.

BETH That's not how I feel—

CURT *(Overlapping.)* You won't even spend the night in my fucking apartment, Beth. You can't stand to be where I live. It's the best I can do and I clean it and clean it and clean it and you still make me come over to your place and it's not because you have to get up early because you don't have to get up that early because you're a fucking artist in the school, for fuck's sake. I mean, what is that? *(Small beat.)* But you won't let me go. I'm not good enough but you won't let me go, you have to have me around. And I keep wondering why because I know it's not because you love me. It's not because I'm the best thing in your life or I make your world or any of that crap. Because you're so fucking hard on me and everybody I know. You hate my friends. And that blows my mind because you have every reason in the world to be nice. Rich people have every reason to be nice—I mean, they live in these huge houses and they drive these huge cars and people fucking kiss their ass every day. And that's why I can't figure out it out. Why is it? Why is it that rich people suck so bad. Why are rich people so fucking mean. Why are they so fucking mean and so fucking selfish and so fucking greedy? I mean, they'll give money away if it gets their name on some building, but they wouldn't give one fucking dime to some bum on the street who's so miserable and so poor that the only joy in his life is standing in some alley sucking back malt liquor. And why not? Are they afraid of making poor people rich? Is that it? Because if that's it, that's not gonna happen. The only thing that would happen is instead of you being rich and me being poor we'd be even. And maybe you'd have to acknowledge that I'm a human being, and if you had to do that, then maybe you couldn't keep treating me like shit! Because if you can't treat me like shit, then you have to face the fact that you fucking suck and you can't face that. And that's why you keep me around. Because you can't feel good about yourself unless there's somebody in the room for you to look down on.

(Long pause.)

BETH Well. Your prostitute friend, I take it, is not rich.

CURT No.

BETH But she fucks the rich. Maybe that's why you like her.

CURT No, she fucks the poor. *(Beat.)* She's just like me. She fucks herself.

The room at the police station. Doug is eating his lunch. Curt enters with a take-out bag.

DOUG What's up? *(Curt sits down.)* Beth called.

CURT What'd you tell her?

DOUG You went to lunch. What's the deal?

CURT We had a fight.

DOUG Over Sandy?

CURT Kind of.

DOUG You should buy Beth some flowers or something. You don't want to lose her. She's a class act. *(Curt doesn't answer.)* I'm reading the paper.

CURT I see that.

DOUG Not just the sports page either. I read the front. Everybody's yelling— *(Finds an article.)* everybody's yelling about how bad the schools are. So they tried to pass this school bond, but nobody voted for it. They want to fix the schools, but they won't pay for it. You know why?

CURT Why?

DOUG Because. They're idiots. They all went to the same

crappy schools as their kids. *(Curt smiles.)* Okay then.

CURT What?

DOUG It's nice to see you with a different expression on

your face. Not looking for once like somebody died.

(Beat.)

CURT Heather's living with you?

DOUG Yeah.

CURT Does it bother you? What she used to do?

DOUG I don't know. I mean, she hates cops, and she's

overlooking that about me. I figure I can do the same for

her. *(Beat.)* Mostly, I just like hanging out with her.

CURT Yeah.

DOUG I went through this, though: I wondered, was she just

so good at faking it, was she faking it with me?

CURT You know there's more to a relationship than sex—

DOUG I'm not talking about sex. I'm talking about the

whole deal. I mean, that's what whores do? Right? They

make you feel good. Even if they hate you, they pretend

like they like you, because that's their job. *(Curt is

troubled.)*

CURT I think Sandy liked me—

DOUG Sure she did. I wasn't saying that.

CURT I think. *(Pause.)* So what else is in the paper?

DOUG Those Christian Coalition freaks are still picketing the massage parlor.

CURT God.

DOUG I heard Bill Horton, though, is going to bust the place.

CURT Where'd you hear that?

DOUG In the bathroom. They got a search warrant or something. I missed some of the details. I totally can't whiz when there's somebody else in the room. Can you?

CURT Has Heather heard from Sandy?

DOUG They're not talking. Something about some boots that got ruined . . . or the stereo. I don't know. We went over there to get Heather's stuff and the place was, like, totally trashed. Like vomit, and shit, everywhere. Somebody flushed something down the toilet and it was backed up all into the carpet. Sandy was like, on her hands and knees, scrubbing the floor, crying. It was sad. We offered to help but she said it was her fault. She didn't want any help.

(Beat.)

CURT Did they say when the raid would be?

DOUG End of the week.

CURT This is the end of the week.

DOUG Could be. *(Curt stands.)* Where you going?

CURT There's a briefing at two. Will you cover for me?

DOUG There is?

CURT Go and cover for me, okay? I owe you. *(He exits.)*

DOUG I owe you more. I mean . . . okay.

*The massage parlor. Sandy is getting dressed. She has on a
bra and panties and is trying to get a stocking hooked back
to a garter. There is money and used Kleenexes and a used
condom on the table. Curt enters.*

CURT Sandy?

SANDY Oh my God.

CURT I need to talk to you.

SANDY I can't believe you're even looking at me. *(She sees
the Kleenex, condom, and money.)* Oh my God. *(She
grabs them, but doesn't know what to do with them.)* I
have a robe. *(She drops them back on the table, grabs a
robe.)*

CURT *(Looking at the mess on the table.)* What is this?

SANDY You know. Are you going to yell at me again?

CURT No. I'm sorry. *(Quick but calm.)* There's going to be
a raid. You don't have to go with me if you don't want, but
you need to leave. There's all those Christians in the
parking lot, so don't go out the front. Use the back.

SANDY *(Nervous.)* They'll think it's weird if I leave early.

CURT Here. *(He pulls out an envelope of money.)* Take

this. Leave now and stay away. Stay away for a couple of

months at least. There's money there. It should hold you.

SANDY I'm not taking money from you.

CURT You can pay me back.

SANDY *(Upset.)* No.

CURT Then don't pay me back. I don't care. Just— I don't

want you to go to jail, okay? I can't think of you there.

SANDY This is not going to make the problem go away.

What do I do after two months?

CURT Maybe you won't want to come back. *(Small beat.)*

Maybe you'll realize you like me enough that you'll do me

the favor of not coming back. Because last time, I thought

maybe that would happen. But I guess . . . were you just

pretending to like me? Because that's what you thought I

wanted?

SANDY No.

CURT If it's just money, if you have to pay bills, then I can

scale back and we can stretch it. You can stay with me as

long as you want. Beth is gone—

SANDY God, I'm sorry.

CURT I don't care, because that means there's nobody else.

There's nobody else who'd care, so why shouldn't we? We can sit. We can be together. Like we were. Just be with each other. *(Beat. Sandy doesn't answer.)* Sandy. I liked being with you.

SANDY Oh God. I liked being with you too.

CURT Then let me do this one thing. Let me do this one thing that I can be proud of.

(They hesitate, then they embrace, holding each other for a long time. Suddenly there is a loud, ugly buzzing, like an intercom. Sandy looks up.)

SANDY The cops are here. Go out the back. Go.

CURT They'll see me.

SANDY Then we'll just—we'll tell them you're here to investigate or something.

CURT They know I'm not.

SANDY Then just tell them you came here to see me. They don't have to know—*(She grabs the money from the table, hers and his.)* Here. Put all the money in your pocket. It's no big deal if you have money. *(Feels the weight of the envelope.)*

CURT Give it here.

SANDY How much is this?

CURT Fifteen hundred.

SANDY *(She pulls the money from the envelope. There's a paper band around it. She looks at the printing on the band.)* What is this?

CURT *(Overlapping. Tries to take it from her.)* Nothing.

SANDY It's an evidence number. *(Small beat.)* You stole evidence?

CURT Look, I didn't have enough in the bank, but I'll get it. I'll get it and put it back and nobody will notice.

SANDY You brought me stolen money—

CURT I'll replace it.

SANDY I thought you wanted us to be together.

CURT I do.

SANDY Where? In jail?

CURT It was a gesture, okay?

SANDY It's a fucking felony!

CURT Just give me back the fucking money! *(He grabs it from her. The buzzer sounds again.)*

SANDY Goddammit. Put the money in your pocket. *(He starts to put the money away.)* Take the band thing off at least, so they don't know where you got it. *(Curt takes it and rips off the band, then shoves the money and the* *band into his pocket. Sandy doesn't see as she goes back to the table and grabs the Kleenex and condom.)* Great. There's a rubber on the table. *(She throws it in the trash, then picks up a Kleenex and wipes off her hands. Curt is watching her when she suddenly stops, self-conscious, and looks at him.)* I have to wipe it off before it dries, okay? It dries like glue. *(Curt doesn't answer.)* You wanted us to live together on stolen money. What sort of stupid fantasy is that?

CURT Mine, okay?

(They watch each other, hurt. The buzzer sounds.)

The room at the massage parlor an hour later. Curt sits in the chair. Doug enters and stands.

DOUG Half the department's out there. *(Beat.)* The lieutenant called and asked me to come down and talk to you.

CURT Uh-huh.

DOUG Um . . . you stole some money?

CURT Yeah.

DOUG Were you gonna return it?

CURT Of course I was. I've never stolen anything in my life.

DOUG I know.

CURT Never in my whole life.

DOUG I know, man. That's why this is so fucked.

(Beat.)

CURT What are they charging me with?

DOUG I don't know yet.

CURT Obstruction of justice, probably. Theft.

DOUG I don't know. It turns out it isn't a raid. It's a search and seizure. They're just looking for financial records.

CURT They're not taking the girls in?

DOUG No. RICO act. They're just seizing the property. They figure you can't have a whorehouse without a house.

CURT Great.

DOUG Everything's under surveillance though. They got everything you said on tape.

(Beat.)

CURT Then I guess all I can do is turn myself in to the lieutenant.

DOUG No.

CURT If I come clean, maybe I could get a reduced sentence—

DOUG No. He's already called somebody from internal affairs. You should call the union and get a lawyer.

CURT I can talk to them by myself.

DOUG No. Call the union and get a lawyer. Now. *(Curt looks at him.)* I can't believe I'm saying this, but, you know. Stop being such a fuck-up. You lost your fiancée and you're probably going to lose your job, but at least you don't have to go to jail. Okay? Try not to ruin your life completely. *(Beat.)* I mean, do you want to go to jail? Seriously?

CURT Does it matter?

DOUG Yes, it matters. Jesus. It's your life and it matters. *(Small beat.)* 'Cause man, you know, you should pay attention to your life. Because I don't want to have to find you someday, just out of prison, maybe with your face cut up, in prison pants. I want to be able to trust you to take care of yourself. So I don't have to find you someday. In a ditch. Maybe high. Maybe naked. *(Beat. Curt barely smiles.)* You got to believe that you deserve the best in this world. Do you believe that?

CURT Sure.

DOUG No. You got to really believe it in your heart, man. Because you do. *(Beat.)* Curt? Buddy? You seriously do.

The bar, a year later. Heather is at the bar, very pregnant. There is a pile of books on the bar next to her, one place over, and one of them is open. She is lazily flipping through it, reading it from where she sits, not really interested. Doug enters, in coat, hat, et cetera. It's very cold outside.

DOUG Sorry I'm late. *(He gives Heather a kiss.)*

HEATHER It's okay.

DOUG I'll run get you dinner.

HEATHER Curt already went.

DOUG Sorry about that.

HEATHER I could've waited, but he said he didn't mind going. How was work?

DOUG You know.

HEATHER Yeah. *(Doug goes behind the bar and gets himself a beer.)* I can't get my coat to zip up over my stomach. I pulled it up here— *(She points below her breasts.)* And I zipped it all the way up but then I couldn't get it down over my stomach. I was walking around with my coat around my head. *(They start laughing.)* I was like, how the fuck am I supposed to drive like this? *(Curt enters with a bag, also in a big coat.)* Oh man. You're a life saver.

CURT No problem.

DOUG Thanks for doing that.

CURT *(Handing the bag to Heather.)* They put the extra cheese in a little thing. On the side.

HEATHER *(Pulling out a container of spaghetti.)* That's great. Oh my God. That smells so good. I get so hungry!

DOUG How much do I owe you?

CURT It's my treat. *(He takes off his coat. Underneath he's wearing a security guard's uniform.)*

DOUG No. How much?

CURT Don't worry about it.

DOUG I'm not letting you pay for it.

CURT I don't mind.

DOUG I mind.

HEATHER *(Leans over the bar and opens the cash register.)* Here. *(She takes out a ten.)* Let's just say it's on the house.

DOUG Excellent. *(Curt takes the ten.)* Beer?

CURT Sure.

HEATHER What is this you're reading? I can't even understand this.

CURT Biology. I don't know.

HEATHER Hey. Do you think babies are born stupid? Or are they born smart?

CURT I don't know. I guess some people are naturally smart.

DOUG Like Doogie Howser.

CURT Like Doogie Howser. Exactly. *(Doug puts a beer on the counter and Curt puts the ten down.)*

HEATHER *(To Doug.)* Don't let him do that.

DOUG What?

HEATHER He'll drink one beer and he'll leave an eight-dollar tip. *(To Curt.)* I can't keep taking eight-dollar tips from you.

CURT Put it in the baby's college fund.

HEATHER I know you can't afford it.

DOUG I'll buy the beer.

CURT You just now didn't have ten dollars. Here. *(Curt shoves the ten toward him.)*

DOUG I'm just going to leave it there. And then it'll end up

back in the cash register. And tell me, where is the justice

in that?

CURT Fine. *(Curt puts the money in his pocket. Sandy*

enters. She is dressed very nicely, very professionally.

She looks great. She's carrying a bright gift bag in pink

and blue. Heather jumps up to greet her. They hug.)

HEATHER Oh my God. What are you doing here?

(Sandy and Curt eye each other.)

SANDY I felt so bad I missed your shower. I wanted to bring

you by your present.

HEATHER That's okay.

DOUG Hey, Sandy.

SANDY Hey, Doug.

(She and Curt look at each other again.)

HEATHER What'd you get me?

SANDY It's for the baby.

(Heather pulls out a little sailor suit.)

HEATHER Oh my God, that is so fucking cute. *(Holding it*

up to Doug.) Did you see that?

DOUG Man, look at that. You know, he could go in the navy.

HEATHER Totally.

DOUG Navy guys are cool.

HEATHER Thank you. *(She hugs Sandy again.)*

SANDY Sure. I mean, you're welcome. Hi, Curt.

CURT Hi.

(Beat.)

DOUG *(To Heather.)* You know, why don't we go in the back room and then you can sit down at a table and eat and . . . stuff.

HEATHER *(Getting it.)* That'd prob'ly be good. *(To Sandy.)* Thanks so much. That was really sweet.

SANDY I'm glad you like it. *(Doug and Heather exit. Sandy stands. Beat.)* I was at the mall last month and I ran into Heather, and I was like, wow, you know, you're pregnant. And we made up and everything.

CURT I didn't even know you were in town.

SANDY I never left.

CURT I didn't know where you were.

SANDY Yeah.

CURT You look great.

SANDY You look good too.

CURT *(Indicates his uniform.)* Rent-a-Cop.

SANDY Where are you working?

CURT Oak Grove Retirement Village.

SANDY Oh. That's nice out there.

CURT It's okay.

SANDY Do you like . . . do security?

CURT I sit at a desk. In the lobby. I work nights, so, it's really quiet.

SANDY That's good.

CURT I guess. I got a second job weekends. At this emergency animal hospital.

SANDY Oh, like as a vet's assistant?

CURT No, just security again. It's in a kind of a bad neighborhood and sometimes drunks come in in the middle of the night. *(Beat.)* What are you doing?

SANDY I have my own business.

CURT Really?

SANDY Yeah. You know, I heard you got fired.

CURT My lawyer cut a deal. I resigned. They didn't press charges. The good thing is, I have a ton of legal bills.

SANDY I'm really sorry. I really messed everything up.

CURT No, you didn't.

SANDY If you hadn't come in—

CURT You didn't do anything. I did it. *(Small beat.)* So what kind of business?

SANDY Same thing. I'm a hooker.

CURT Oh.

SANDY It's funny, because when they closed down the massage parlor, I was like, what am I going to do now? You know? I was really depressed and I didn't have any money and my landlord was going to evict me. And then I thought, you know, if I'm just sitting around my house, I bet all those johns are just sitting around their houses too. 'Cause, the guys that came to us, they don't want to pick up whores on the street. You know? They want a certain level of quality, they want a certain level of cleanliness, and they don't want to barter. They want a set fee structure. So I figured what the hell, I'd see what happened, and I put an ad in the *Press-Citizen*, in the personals, just saying, you know, "Professional masseuse, formerly of Naughty But Nice, looking for that special someone in search of a good time." It was one of those deals where you get a voice mailbox at the paper, right? And it ran on a Thursday, and Thursday night my voice

mail was totally full. Totally full. I couldn't believe it. And
half the guys I knew. So I just went with the guys I knew.
I started there, charging the same prices so they wouldn't
feel ripped off. And I told them, if you have friends, and
you want to recommend me, great. And now I have a full
client list. Very private. I won't take anybody without a
recommendation. And I moved. I got a townhouse over in
Glenwood Estates—

CURT That's really nice.

SANDY There's some overhead and I have to do my own
scheduling, of course, but I have my mornings free and at
the end of the day, I'm my own boss. I get a hundred
percent of the profits and hopefully I can retire by the
time I'm thirty.

(Pause.)

CURT I took this job because I wanted to work nights. And
I knew there wasn't a lot to it. In fact, I make my rounds
every hour, takes me about ten minutes and then I've got
the rest of the hour free—

SANDY That's great.

CURT I was thinking that'd be good because I'm in school

now. And I thought I could get a lot of reading done at
night. But I found out right away that they absolutely will
not allow you to read on the job. They even check the
tape from the security cameras. To make sure you're not
doing anything you're not supposed to. So for fifty
minutes out of every hour, I basically sit there. *(Long
pause. He takes a drink of his beer.)*

SANDY You're in school?

CURT Yeah. I'm going to Kirkwood. Community College.

SANDY That's great.

CURT All the state schools rejected me. Can you believe
that?

SANDY No.

CURT I didn't have anybody to ask for a recommendation.

SANDY But the community college took you.

CURT Yeah. Well. It turns out they have open admissions, so
they have to take everybody.

SANDY That's great.

CURT I wanted to take forestry classes, but they don't offer
any. So I'm taking biology. Which is the closest thing they
have. But I'm not really learning anything. The guy who's

teaching it is like one chapter ahead of us in the textbook. He's just an adjunct. He doesn't have office hours. He doesn't even have an office.

SANDY But you're doing good, right?

CURT Well. No. I did okay in math, but anything where I have to write a paper, it's like, I have the idea but I don't know how to write it out. If I could talk it instead of write it, I'd be fine. But I can't make it sound right on paper. I get the stupid things back and it's just red marks everywhere. Awkward awkward awkward awkward.

(Beat.) But, you know, it's what I always wanted to do.

SANDY That's great.

CURT That's the fourth time you've said that.

SANDY What?

CURT That's what you said. To your cousin who glued the triangles together. You smiled and said that's great but you knew, deep down inside, that it was never going to happen.

(Beat.)

SANDY I'm sorry.

(Beat.)

CURT You shouldn't be sorry. *(Pause. Curt finishes*

his beer. He pats Sandy's hand.) It was good to see

you.

SANDY *(Quickly.)* Are you still learning your leaves?

CURT I don't know. I try.

SANDY I stole one from you.

CURT What?

SANDY I didn't know if you'd notice. But I stole one from

you. I put it under my shirt that night and I took it home. I

put it up . . . I taped it in my window. In my kitchen. I

look at it in the mornings. While I drink my coffee.

CURT Which one?

SANDY Ironwood.

CURT *Ostrya virginica.*

SANDY It's not fancy—

CURT No. But it's a good tree. It's a little tree.

SANDY Yeah?

CURT Grows under the canopy.

SANDY Anyway, I like it.

CURT I don't know if I'll get to be a guide now.

SANDY Why not?

CURT I lost my pension. When I lost my job. So I don't
know about retiring.

SANDY Oh.

CURT But I didn't know you did that. That you took a leaf.
I'm glad you did.

SANDY Yeah. *(Long pause.)*

CURT You know, I think I just got tired.

SANDY I know.

CURT All those years and all that work. I didn't throw it
away on you.

SANDY I know.

CURT I got so mad and I threw it away on feeling sorry for
myself. I never did that before. And all I can figure is, I
just got tired. *(Beat.)* But no more of that. I'm going to
get my grades up. I'm going to be grateful I don't have a
record.

SANDY That's . . . I think that sounds great.

CURT Yeah. Now when I find myself feeling tired . . . like
right now, actually, right now I feel tired, seeing you . . .
(He might cry.)

SANDY I should go.

CURT But when I find myself feeling tired now, I just stop and I say to myself, "You know, if you don't take care of yourself, Curt, who else will?" You know? And I think about— I think about how I'm going to be the godfather to that kid in there. . . .

SANDY Yeah?

CURT And I think, "What kind of role model do you want to be?" *(Small beat.)* And that's what does it. *(Beat.)* That's what does it. For me, anyway. *(Beat. He's crying. Sandy looks uncertain, then she holds out her hand.)*

SANDY I could hold your hand for just a little while.

CURT What?

SANDY If you want, I could sit here for just a little while, and I could hold your hand. *(Beat.)* If you want. *(Curt looks at her, hesitates, then gives her his hand. She takes it. They sit on the bar stools, side by side, and look toward something outside themselves that they can't quite see.)*

LIGHTS FADE